INCREDIBLE INSURANCE CLAIMS

BY BRIAN HERBERT

Cover Painting
and Illustrations
by Ed Powers

PRICE/STERN/SLOAN
Publishers, Inc., Los Angeles

1982

DEDICATION

To the stalwart claims adjuster whose job it is to be all things to all people. In comparison, the chameleon sitting on a scotch plaid has an easy task. The claims adjuster is simultaneously a chisler to the claimant, a snail to the agent, and a spendthrift to the home office. His accomplishments call upon him to display the talents of a lawyer, a doctor, an accountant, and a clairvoyant with a dash of bloodhound.

Published by Price/Stern/Sloan Publishers, Inc.
410 North La Cienega Boulevard, Los Angeles, California 90048

ISBN: 0-8431-0309-4

Library of Congress Catalog Card Number: 81-85642

INTRODUCTION

It would be difficult for even an accomplished writer to match the comedy provided by people identified herein as The Insured and The Claimant. Almost as if they were characters in a play, they find themselves in improbable episodes which end in claims best described as testimonials to chutzpah.

Certain names, dates, and facts have been changed in order to protect the innocent and the not so innocent.

The accident occurred when the woman driving the car attempted to remove her girdle and lost control of the vehicle.

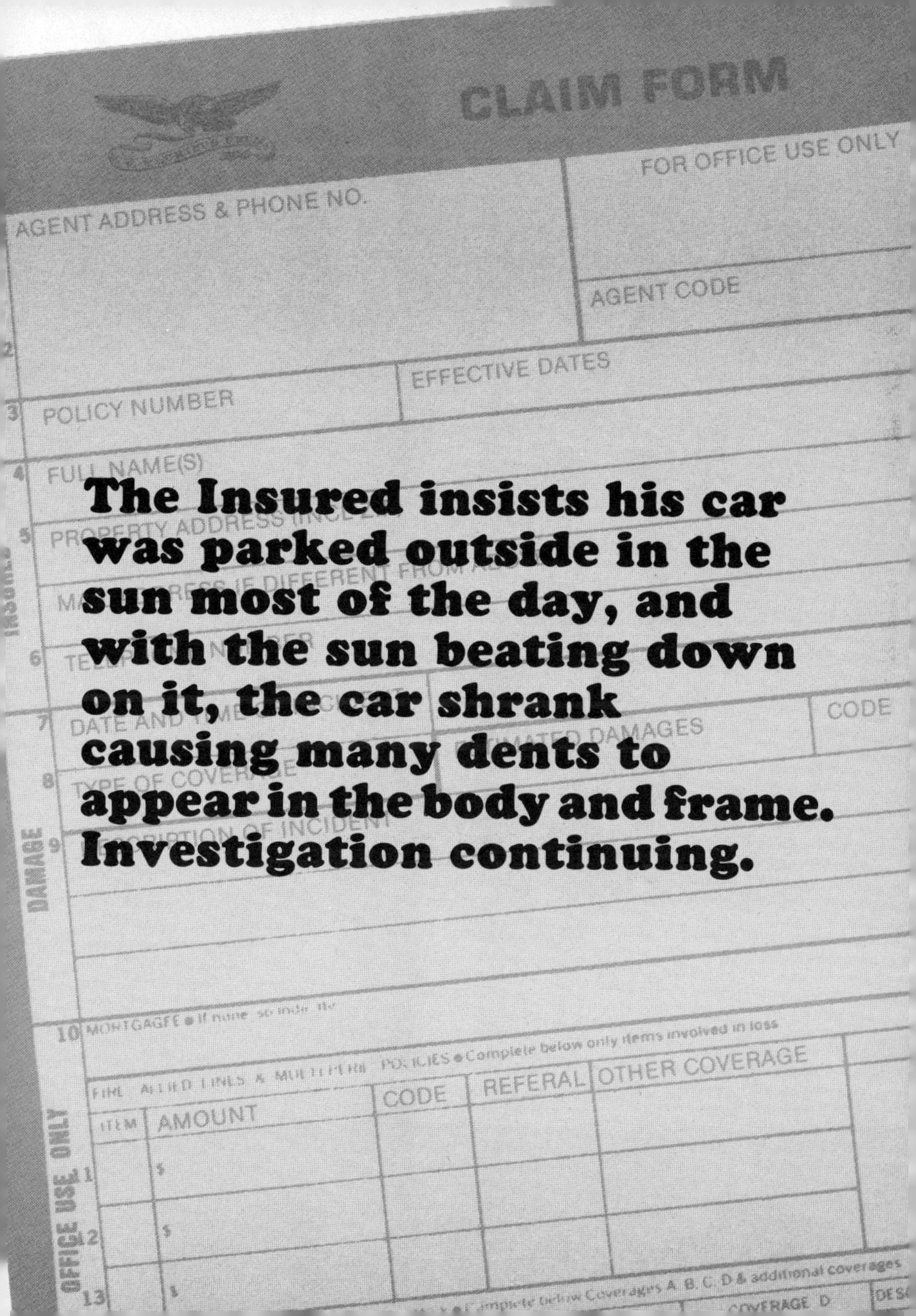

The Insured insists his car was parked outside in the sun most of the day, and with the sun beating down on it, the car shrank causing many dents to appear in the body and frame. Investigation continuing.

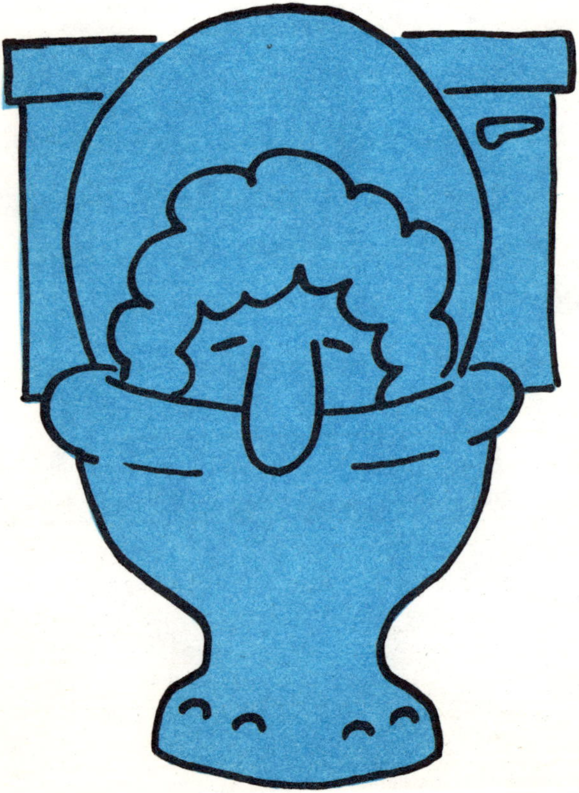

INTER-OFFICE MEMO

Date 9-18-81

Subject: The insured was ill and vomiting in the toilet when the lid fell down on her, breaking her nose. We told her there was no coverage for this.

FROM THE DESK OF: J.J. Gibbons

INSURED'S STATEMENT:

"The telephone pole was approaching. I attempted to move out of its way, but it hit me!"

. . . Apparently the hitch-hiker had been administering oral sex to the driver at the time of the accident.

PHONE MEMO

DATE 6-21-81

TIME 10:20 AM PM

AREA CODE—TELEPHONE NO.—OR OPER.

EXTENSION #

TO: Ed P.

FROM: Bob L.

RE: Policy #276N403P

Mrs. Hampsted reports that birds near her house have been getting drunk on mountain ash berries. Two drunken birds crashed through the bedroom window and stayed just long enough to ruin her bedspread. Does Homeowner Policy cover birds and bedspreads?

AGENT Roger B.

INSURED NAS-409

POLICY DATE 6-1-80

FOR OFFICE USE ONLY

Our insured is seeking $100,000 in damages caused when he fell through the rotten floor of a state-owned outhouse and nearly drowned in the waste-filled tank below. According to the Game Warden of the area, a sign had been posted, warning that the facility was closed, but vandals had probably removed the sign. Liability to be determined.

Mrs. Sanders was wearing her leopard-skin coat in the parking lot of Southeastern Shopping Center. She says that an ocelot jumped out from behind a pickup truck, attacked the coat, and ran off.

The Claimant stated he was giving a speech at a convention before several hundred people. While walking around on the stage, his pants zipper fell, allegedly causing him extreme embarrassment and loss of prestige. Our Insured manufactured the slacks.

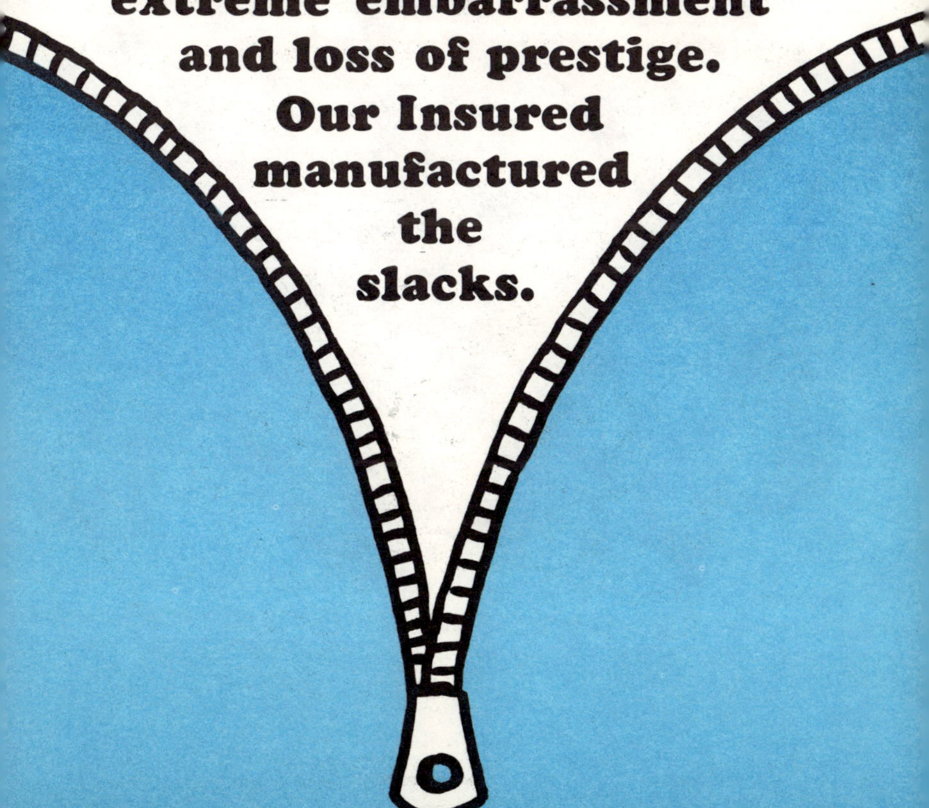

BE DAMAGE TO VEH.

CIRCLE ONE OF THE 8 DIAGRAMS BELOW IF IT ADEQUATELY DESCRIBES THE ACCIDENT OR DRAW YOUR OWN DIAGRAM IN THE SPACE TO THE RIGHT

REAR END	RIGHT TURN
OVERTAKING	RIGHT TURN
LEFT TURN	HEAD ON
INTERSECTION	SIDESWIPE

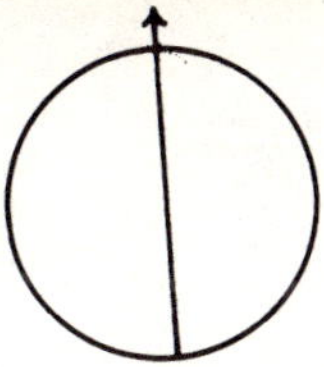

INDICATE NORTH

ACCIDENT DESCRIPTION Our investigation indicates that just prior to the accident, Ms. Johnson, while driving:
1. Placed her right hand upon the dashboard in order to receive a manicure from the passenger.
#2. Began brushing her teeth with her left hand.
#3. Attempted to steer the vehicle with her left elbow.
INVESTIGATION CONTINUING.

Injury Section: Fill Out Space Below for Every Person In

Date of Report

SIGN HERE

INSURED'S STATEMENT:

"I knocked over a man. He admitted it was his fault as he has been run over before."

INSURED'S STATEMENT:

"The indirect cause of this accident was a little guy in a small car with a big mouth."

"I was taking my canary to the vet. It got loose in the car and flew out the window. The next thing I saw was his rear end and there was a crash."

"In my attempt to kill a fly, I drove into a telephone pole."

TO

The office of
the Fire Chief

INFORMATION REQUESTED:

Clarification of circumstances regarding station-house fire.

REPLY:

A fire dept. employee lit two logs in the office fireplace. He didn't realize that the fireplace was fake, and almost burned the building down.

". . . he parked just outside a circus tent. Somehow an elephant got loose and sat on the hood of his car."

INCIDENT REPORT
CLAIMS DIVISION – HOME OFFI

ORIGIN: Southern Office

POLICY # H-6007-PI

DATE OF INDIDENT: May 25, 1980

TIME OF INCIDENT: 2:30 P.M.

In order to dry her poodle, The Insured placed the dog in a microwave oven and set the oven on full power for ten minutes. The dog exploded, throwing glass from the microwave door and poodle parts all over the kitchen. The Insured refuses to return to the house until it has been cleaned, and is charging hotel bills to the agent at the rate of $85 per day.

FFICE COPY ONLY

OUR INSURED WAS SITTING IN HIS APARTMENT LISTENING TO A RECORDING OF "CRY OF THE WILD GOOSE" WHEN A LIVE MALE GOOSE SMASHED THROUGH THE LIVING ROOM WINDOW

"I GOT UP IN THE MORNING TO GO TO WORK. I WENT INTO THE BATHROOM AND WAS SPRAYING MY HAIR WITH HAIRSPRAY WHEN THE SPRAYER STUCK OPEN. I COULD NOT GET IT TO QUIT SPRAYING, SO I HELD THE CAN OVER THE TOILET AND EXPELLED THE REST OF THE SPRAY. THEN I THREW THE CAN AWAY. LATER MY HUSBAND CAME HOME, SAT DOWN ON THE TOILET AND LIT A CIGARETTE. HE WAS BLOWN INTO THE BATHROOM WALL, BREAKING HIS COLLAR BONE, FOR WHICH WE ARE ENTERING A CLAIM."

The Insured explained that he was not at the wheel when his auto service truck crashed into a car he was about to tow. "My dog Booger was at the wheel," he said. "I always trade places with him when I have to operate the car lift."

IT ACTUALLY HAPPENED

The Insured operates a dude ranch and we insure all of his ranch buildings and his pickup truck. He had been having trouble with coyotes and had rigged up an ingenious sapling cage trap to catch the animals, after which he would shoot them. This time he decided to try something different, and instead of shooting the coyote, he tied a stick of dynamite to its neck and lit the fuse, opening the cage door at the same time. The coyote unobligingly ran under The Insured's pickup truck. The claim is for the truck which is a total loss.

"My guns, a coin collection, two diamond rings, and a snowmobile were stolen sometime during the night!!"

"I'm sorry, Mr. Powers . . . they took all of your exclusions."

"The squirrel broke into my house, and apparently was unable to find food. So it chomped up my window mouldings and spit them all over the place before drowning itself in the toilet."

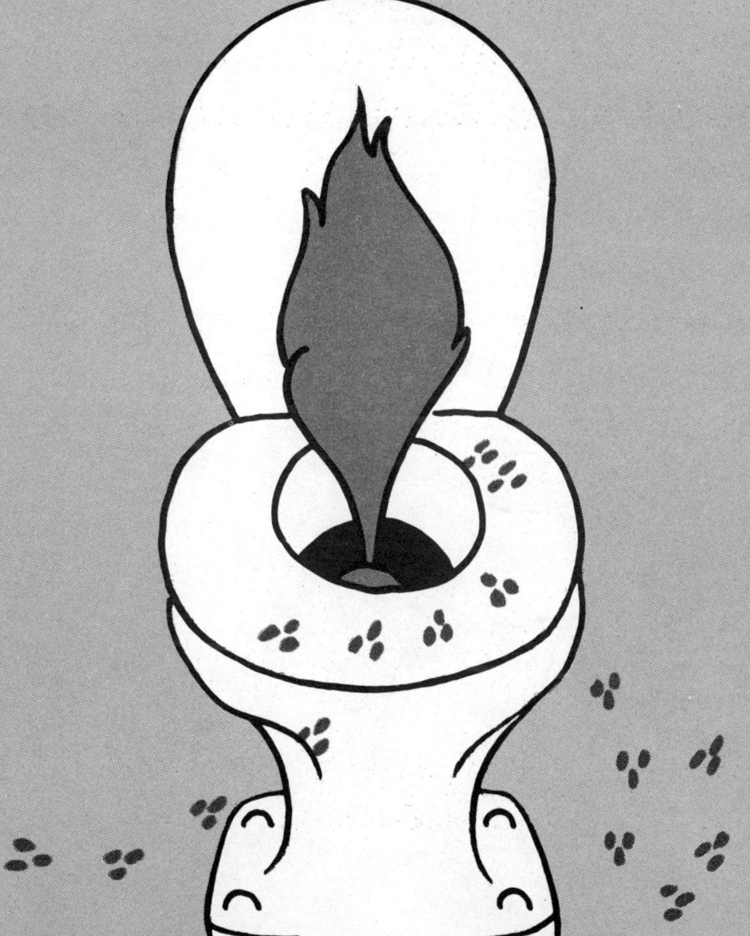

"Whenever I get angry, I close my eyes and count to ten. I was mad at my brother while driving on the expressway and closed my eyes. The next thing I knew there was a terrible crash."

. . . and we insure the manufacturing company. According to the complaint, Plaintiff suffered mental anguish when one of their burial vaults leaked, allegedly resulting in damage to the corpse of his loved one. We are establishing a reserve in the event of an adverse judgement.

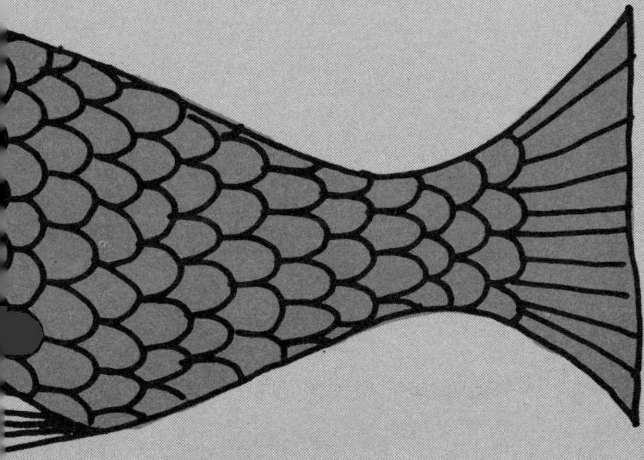

FIELD REPORT

CLAIM: 3-98440-NP

ORIGIN: Montana Branch

INVESTIGATOR'S STATEMENT:

Claimant has filed for reimbursement on behalf of her husband who expired due to an alleged heart attack while on business for his company. Investigation and evidence reveal, however, that the deceased actually expired while attempting to make love to a Shetland pony. It appears that the deceased was driving by a pasture outside Northern Montana and saw the pony grazing. During their interlude, part of the salesman's ear was bitten off by the pony. It is of my opinion that the claim should be denied.

Signed [signature]

Date 3-18-'81

The Insured was fishing at Cold Springs Harbor and hooked a large fish. The fish, however, swam off with her rod and reel.

Her claim is for theft.

Intending to test her new smoke detector, the tenant lit a match beneath the device. It worked. Unfortunately, she then threw the lit match into a trash container, igniting the contents. Total damage is estimated at $50,000.

DESCRIPTION OF INCIDENT

Describe fully how accident happened, illustrating when practicable by a sketch.

I was playing pool against a girl and it was her shot at the eight ball. I was standing by the pocket she was shooting at. I had my hand on the side of the pocket, but she didn't make it and she said I made her miss. We talked for a minute. I was trying to say I didn't make you miss but she wouldn't listen. Then she told me to kiss her B-hind. I said you show it, then she bent over and I kicked her in the end, and she picked up the pool rack and hit me in the head. Then we started fighting but they broke it up.

Signed [signature]

Date MAR. 13, 1981

IT ACTUALLY HAPPENED

The artist reported there was a bug on his leg so he drew his pistol and shot it. Unfortunately, he also shot a hole in his foot.

The Insured's claim is that his neighbor's children knocked out all the knot-holes in his fence.

MORE INCREDIBLE STATEMENTS BY CLAIMANTS:

"I pulled away from the side of the road, glanced at my mother-in-law, and headed over the embankment."

DESCRIBE INCIDENT:

Suspect drove her vehicle into

. . . eighteen parked cars, four moving vehicles, two stop signs, one trailer truck,

between Sycamore and Rose Avenues.

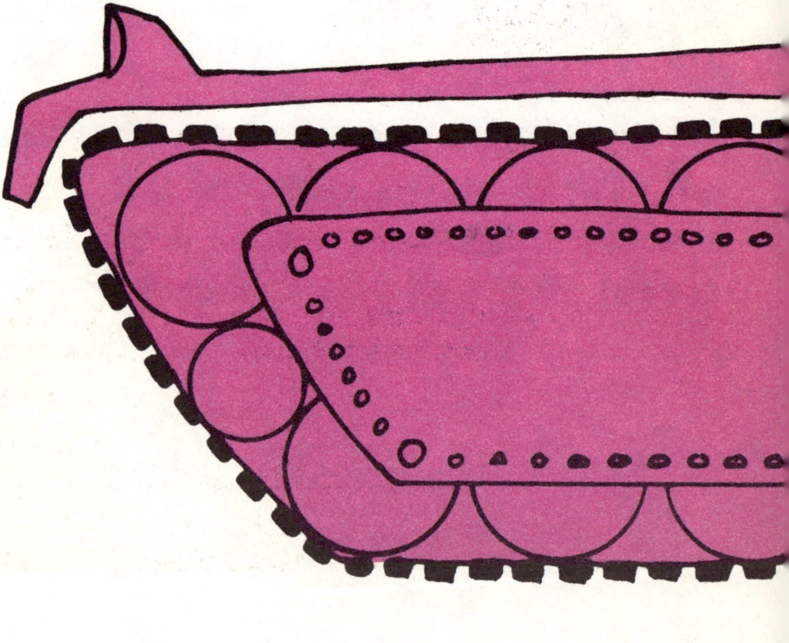

Suspect's statement:
I was mad at my boyfriend.

Gentlemen:

This morning I bought a bottle of your soda and found a thing floating in it. This has caused me considerable mental pain, for which I wish to enter a claim. I am holding the bottle, unopened, and would like you to have your insurance adjuster look at it with an eye to a settlement before whatever is in the bottle dissolves and I won't have the evidence to show.

R. Smith

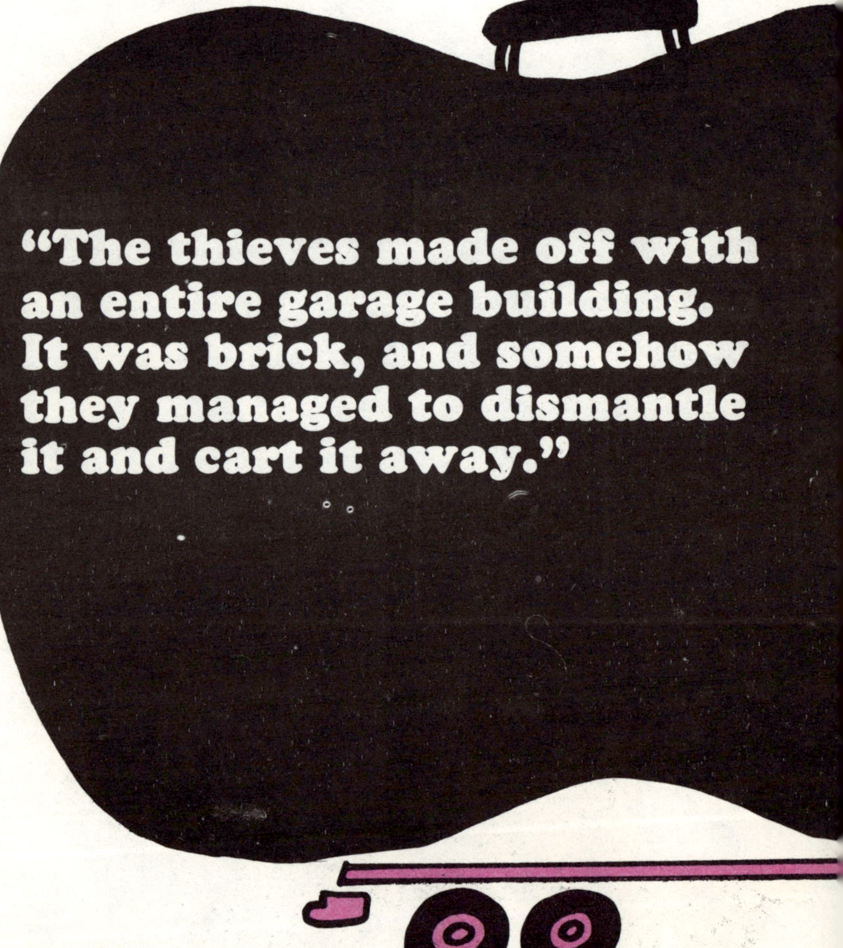

"The thieves made off with an entire garage building. It was brick, and somehow they managed to dismantle it and cart it away."

LINES INSURANCE COMPANIES CHERISH

The driver explained she was trying to make an "O" turn. When the adjuster looked mystified she explained,

"That's a "U" turn where you change your mind."

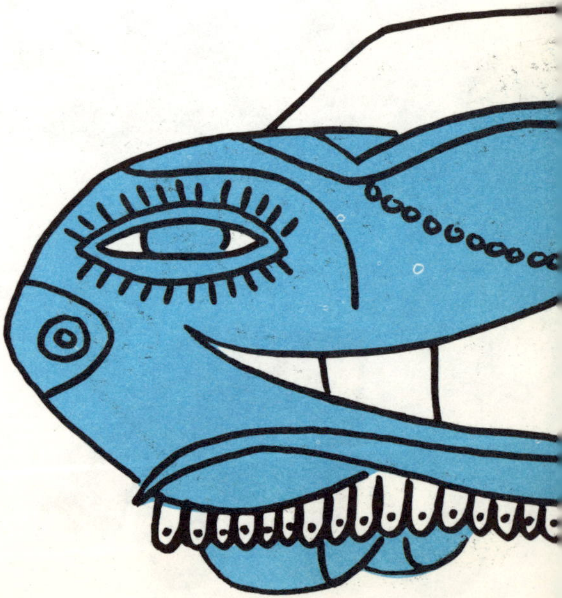

A woman dented the rear fender of another car while attempting to park her own. A question on the accident report asked her what could have been done to prevent the accident.

She wrote, "He could have parked somewhere else."

This book is published by

PRICE/STERN/SLOAN
Publishers, Inc., Los Angeles

whose other splendid titles include such literary classics as:

ART AFTERPIECES ($3.95)
LEGAL GUIDE TO MOTHER GOOSE ($2.50)
MURPHY'S LAW AND
OTHER REASONS WHY THINGS GO ƆNOЯW! (2.95)
MURPHY'S LAW/BOOK TWO ($2.95)
I DON'T GET NO RESPECT ($1.75)
THE PROFIT ($2.50)

and many, many more

They are available wherever books are sold, or may be ordered directly from the publisher by sending check or money order for total abount plus $1.00 for handling and mailing. For a complete list of titles send a *stamped, self-addressed envelope* to:

PRICE/STERN/SLOAN *Publishers, Inc.*
410 North La Cienega Boulevard, Los Angeles, California 90048